Create and Share | Thinking Digitally

Respecting Others Online

By Ann Truesdell

Published in the United States of America by:

CHERRY LAKE PRESS

2395 South Huron Parkway, Suite 200, Ann Arbor, Michigan
www.cherrylakepublishing.com

Series Adviser: Kristin Fontichiaro
Reading Adviser: Marla Conn, MS, Ed., Literacy specialist, Read-Ability, Inc.
Book Designer: Felicia Macheske
Character Illustrator: Rachael McLean

Photo Credits: © Akkalak Aiempradit/Shutterstock.com, 7; © Hrytsiv Oleksandr/Shutterstock.com, 13; © Morrowind/
Shutterstock.com, 14

Graphics Throughout: © the simple surface/Shutterstock.com; © Diana Rich/Shutterstock.com; © lemony/Shutterstock.com;
© CojoMoxon/Shutterstock.com; © IreneArt/Shutterstock.com; © Artefficient/Shutterstock.com; © Marie Nimrichterova/Shutterstock.
com; © Svetolk/Shutterstock.com; © EV-DA/Shutterstock.com; © briddy/Shutterstock.com; © Mix3r/Shutterstock.com

Library of Congress Cataloging-in-Publication Data

Names: Truesdell, Ann, author. | McLean, Rachael, illustrator.
Title: Respecting others online / by Ann Truesdell ; illustrated by Rachael McLean.
Description: Ann Arbor, Michigan : Cherry Lake Publishing, 2020. | Series:
Create and share : thinking digitally | Includes index. | Audience:
Grades 2-3.
Identifiers: LCCN 2019033408 (print) | LCCN 2019033409 (ebook) |
ISBN 9781534159075 (hardcover) | ISBN 9781534161375 (paperback) |
ISBN 9781534160224 (pdf) | ISBN 9781534162525 (ebook)
Subjects: LCSH: Online etiquette—Juvenile literature. | Respect—Juvenile
literature.
Classification: LCC TK5105.878 .T7833 2020 (print) | LCC TK5105.878
(ebook) | DDC 395.5—dc23
LC record available at https://lccn.loc.gov/2019033408
LC ebook record available at https://lccn.loc.gov/2019033409

Cherry Lake Publishing would like to acknowledge the work of the Partnership for 21st Century Learning, a Network of Battelle
for Kids. Please visit *www.battelleforkids.org/networks/p21* for more information.

Printed in the United States of America
Corporate Graphics

CHERRY LAKE PRESS

Table of
CONTENTS

CHAPTER ONE

Respect in Real Life

We are all part of a community, from classrooms to countries. Communities work best when people treat each other with respect. When we respect other people, we show that we care about their feelings and safety. Respectful behavior creates a good community.

When you are respectful, you use basic manners like saying "please" and "thank you." You hold the door open for others. You pick up trash to keep your environment clean. You listen when others are speaking and wait your turn to talk. These are all ways that we show respect.

Many people are also part of **online** communities. Showing respect online looks a little different from showing respect in the real world. But the same rules apply. When you are communicating online, think about what you would do or say in real life. If you would never say something to a person face-to-face, then you probably shouldn't say it online either. Treat people with respect both online and offline!

Treat others how you would like to be treated.

Is This Respectful?

Paul is not always respectful online. For each example below, consider how he could change his behavior to be more respectful.

- When someone bothers Paul in an online game, he responds by calling them rude names.
- SOMETIMES, PAUL LIKES TO TYPE IN ALL CAPS.
- A friend sends Paul a text message that says something nice about him. Paul types back "whatever."
- Paul posts silly pictures of his cousin online without asking her permission.

Why do you think these examples were disrespectful?
Read the next chapter to find out!

We show respect in real life many different ways.
How do we show respect online?

CHAPTER TWO

Online Etiquette

There are many different ways that people show respect when they are online. Talking to a person online is different from talking to a person face-to-face. So people use special rules for polite online behavior.

In real life, people can see each other's facial expressions. They can hear each other's tone of voice. Online, the other person can only read what is written. This is why many people use **emojis**. Adding an emoji can help.

Another special rule for writing online is to avoid using all capital letters, called "all caps." When you type a message in all caps, it is considered YELLING! You only want to use all caps when you REALLY want to emphasize certain words.

You should respect other people's privacy as well as your own. When you meet new people online, consider how you would talk to a stranger in real life. It would not be safe for you to give a stranger **private** information, like your last name, address, and birthdate. It would also be rude to ask another person for their private information.

Sometimes people tease their friends when they are face-to-face. But this usually doesn't work out very well online! Things that might be funny to say in person can look mean when typed out. It is difficult to show your expressions and friendly tone of voice through text, even with emojis. When you are online, you have to consider your words carefully. Try a friendly compliment instead!

People should also respect their real-life friends online. Have you ever taken a silly picture of a friend? That picture may be fine on your phone. But you should never share it online without your friend's permission. You also want to avoid posting any information about your friends. It's like talking about your friends when they are not there, which isn't very nice or respectful.

There are benefits to communicating through writing. You can often reread what you've written before you send or post. This gives you the chance to make sure that you said what you wanted to say, in a respectful way.

Ask Permission

When you are sharing things with others online, it is very important to be careful with your words and actions. Consider this example:

You decide to surprise your friend Paul with a video on YouTube for his birthday. You put a lot of photos of him in the video. You include his school picture and a silly photo of him wearing his little sister's tutu. You include a **voice-over** that says:

"Paul Adan is a pretty cool kid at Jefferson Elementary School. He gets good grades and is awesome at soccer. I can't wait for your birthday party, Paul! Have a good one!"

When Paul watches the video, he gets mad. What did you do wrong? What could you have done differently?

CHAPTER THREE

Rude Is Not Respectful

Most people try to be kind online, but there are some people who do mean things. They often do this for the same reasons they are mean in real life. They might think that being mean will make them look tough to other people. Or they could be having a bad day.

There are many ways people are unkind online. **Trolls** can ruin online games and communities by annoying or bothering other people. **Hackers** might try to break into other people's **accounts**. People sometimes get upset and "shout" or use bad words. If you are bothered by these people online, it is best to ignore them. You can also report them in the game or website if they continue to bother you.

If an online conversation is getting out of hand, sign out.

Internet trolls are looking to start a fight for their own entertainment. They might not even mean what they post. They are just trying to make you mad!

The most serious kind of disrespect that can happen online is **cyberbullying**. Sometimes cyberbullies send messages to people. Other times they post about people on public websites for others to read. If you or a friend is being cyberbullied, talk to a trusted adult about it right away.

Harmless or Hurtful?

Sometimes, people accidentally hurt other people's feelings online. When you send a message, be sure your words are respectful and polite. Before you press Send or Post, reread what you have written. Does your message include kind words? Will the person receiving your message understand your jokes or teasing? Is this something that would be better said in person?

For the examples below, decide if the messages are respectful or rude.

- *Hey. Do you think you can bring back that game you borrowed? You forgot last time.*
- *I'm so lost in math. Help me? You always seem to know everything.*
- *Congratulations on the award. You must have been so surprised.*
- *Don't forget to bring my sweater.*

Try reading the messages out loud in different voices. First, try reading in a nice tone. Then, try again in a rude voice. The tone of the message changed based on the voice you used. These messages aren't necessarily rude, but they can come across that way. What can you add or change to the message to make it clearly respectful? Would you add exclamation points? What about a "please" or "thank you?"

There is nothing wrong with being new to a game.
But calling someone a "noob" or "newb" is rude.
It's like telling them they are bad at the game.

CHAPTER FOUR

Disconnect from the Disrespect

Trolls, hackers, and cyberbullies can make the internet a frustrating place. But there are ways to **overcome** those negative users.

It's important to talk to an adult you trust when something makes you sad, hurt, scared, or uncomfortable. This is true in both real life and online. Adults can help you sort out your feelings and find the best solution for your problem.

Sometimes the solution is to report or **block** others. Reporting or blocking other users gives them a warning that they are doing something unacceptable. If they continue their bad behavior, they may get kicked out of a game or banned from a site.

Other times, you might have to get away from the disrespectful person. You may need to switch to a different game. Or you may need to go offline for a while.

If you see someone else getting disrespected online, you can help them by being an **upstander**. Upstanders stick up for other people, even if they don't know them in real life. Upstanders let the person being bullied know that someone is on their side.

The best way to get rid of cyberbullies or trolls is to block or report them.

ACTIVITY

It is helpful to have a plan for dealing with tough situations before they happen. Below, match the online problem with the best solution. There may be more than one solution to a problem.

ONLINE PROBLEMS

1. A stranger asks for your age and address online
2. Someone in a game calls you dumb
3. A kid from school won't stop posting rude comments on your posts
4. Your account has been hacked
5. Someone is calling another player bad names in a game

SOLUTIONS

A. Tell the other person to stop

B. Ignore the other person

C. Tell a trusted adult

D. Report or block the other person

E. Switch to a different game or server

F. Take a break from being online

G. Change your password

Why did you choose the solutions that you did? Discuss your thoughts with a friend or an adult. There are many right answers!

If you are standing up for someone, be careful not to get into a **flame war** with the bully.

GLOSSARY

accounts (uh-KOUNTS) requirements that some websites have where they ask for your personal information before allowing you into the site, like a username and password

block (BLAHK) to prevent someone online from contacting you

cyberbullying (SYE-bur-bul-ee-ing) the act of bullying someone online

emojis (ih-MOH-jeez) small images or symbols used in text messages or online to express emotions

flame war (FLAME WOR) angry messages between online users

hackers (HAK-urz) people who secretly gain access to an account

online (AWN-line) connected to the internet

overcome (oh-vur-KUHM) to get control of a problem

private (PRYE-vit) belonging to only one person or group of people and not shared with anyone else

trolls (TROHLZ) people who purposely are rude to others online

upstander (UP-stand-ur) person who stands up for others who are being bullied

voice-over (VOIS-oh-vur) the voice of someone unseen speaking

BOOKS

Hubbard, Ben. *My Digital Rights and Rules*. Minneapolis, Minnesota: Lerner Publications, 2018.

Nickel, Scott. *Be Kind Online: A Garfield Guide to Online Etiquette*. Minneapolis, Minnesota: Lerner Publications Group, Inc., 2020

WEBSITES

BrainPOP—Digital Etiquette
https://www.brainpop.com/technology/digitalcitizenship/digitaletiquette
Learn more about how to be respectful online.

Wonderopolis—What is Digital Citizenship?
https://www.wonderopolis.org/wonder/what-is-digital-citizenship
Discover what it means to be a good digital citizen.

INDEX

About the AUTHOR

Ann Truesdell is a school librarian in Michigan. She and her husband, Mike, are the proud parents of James, Charlotte, Matilda, and Alice. They all enjoy reading, traveling, being outside, and spending time with their dog, Leia.